Northumberlan
Durham Railway Pictorial
1948–1967
Brian J. Dickson

Contents

Every effort has been made to trace copyright holders of the photographs reproduced. Apologies are offered to any who may have been missed.

©Kestrel Railway Books and Brian J. Dickson 2010

Kestrel Railway Books
PO Box 269
SOUTHAMPTON
SO30 4XR

www.kestrelrailwaybooks.co.uk

Printed by The Amadeus Press

ISBN 978-1-905505-20-3

Front cover: 1953. Class J21 0-6-0 65033 brings a Gresley BSK over the Border Counties bridge on the approach to Hexham. *(Colour-Rail.com/BRE218)*

Back cover, top: July 1966. Class J27 0-6-0 65838 brings a single brake van past Winning signalbox. *(M Covey-Crump/Colour-Rail.com/BRE2187)*

Back cover, bottom: September 1966. Class J27 0-6-0 65842 in ex-works condition is seen at Woodburn with the Thursdays-only freight from Morpeth. *(John M Boyes/Colour-Rail.com/BRE222)*

Title Page: Friday 11th August 1950. A classic period scene with as yet un-named class A1 4-6-2 No 60157 departing Newcastle with a train for London. This particular locomotive was built in 1949 at Doncaster works, and would be named *Great Eastern* in 1951. She would be withdrawn from service in 1965. *(Eric Treacy)*

Left: Monday 22nd April 1963. With a heavy train of coal wagons from Hylton Colliery, ex-NER class P3 (LNER J27) 0-6-0 No 65854 struggles to restart on the gradient adjacent to Southwick goods station. This locomotive was built by Beyer Peacock in 1908, and would be withdrawn from service only eight months after this photograph was taken at the end of 1963. *(IS Carr)*

Introduction

Northumberland and Durham, Steel, Coal and Shipbuilding, these two counties and the three great industries are forever linked. With some of the earliest recorded coal mining and iron smelting activities taking place in the counties, and the growth of shipbuilding during the 19th and early 20th centuries on the rivers Tyne, Wear and Tees, it is hardly surprising that the railways grew apace to service the expansion brought about by these industries in the North East.

By the time that the railways were nationalised at the beginning of January 1948, coal was still being transported in huge quantities by rail from the many collieries in the two counties to power stations near Newcastle and to ports, harbours and docks on the North Sea coast for export. In Durham, the docks at Hartlepool and South Shields and the forest of coal staithes at Seaham harbour were the most prominent, and in Northumberland, the coal staithes at Blyth were one of the largest facilities for the shipment of coal in the North East.

Coal was also being transported inland, primarily to the coking plants that served the massive steel works at Consett. Established in 1840 as an iron works, it grew steadily using local supplies of coal, iron ore and limestone until the 1880s when steel production was introduced. Rapid growth followed, with iron ore being imported from northern Spain through Tyne Dock. This traffic required powerful locomotives to haul the heavy trains, and many ex-NER class T3 (LNER class Q7) 0-8-0s were allocated to Tyne Dock depot for a large part of their working lives. In the mid-1950s, ten of the then new BR Standard class 9F 2-10-0s were allocated there to handle these heavy trains, and they continued to do so until 1966, when they were withdrawn, and the haulage of the trains passed to BR/Sulzer type 2s working in pairs.

During 1951, British Railways introduced 56-ton gross bogie hopper wagons on the Tyne Dock-Consett iron ore trains. Initially used in eight-wagon rakes for haulage by the class Q7s, this was increased to nine wagons during 1956 when the Standard class 9Fs were introduced to the service.

Railway ownership in Northumberland and Durham was not only in the hands of British Railways. The National Coal Board (NCB) had been formed exactly a year prior to BR, and the railways associated with the collieries and workings acquired by them spread web-like across the countryside, providing access from the collieries to exchange sidings, and in some cases, directly to ports and docks. One of the largest systems that became part of the NCB was that of the Lambton, Hetton & Joicey Collieries (LH&JC), which had its locomotive depot and extensive workshop complex at Philadelphia, near Chester-le-Street. With almost 70 miles of railways, it used a wide variety of locomotives from pre-grouping 0-6-0 tender types to purpose-built 0-6-2 tanks by Kitson & Co; the use of steam traction here continued until early in 1969.

In contrast to all the heavy industry in these counties, many branch lines served rural communities in both Northumberland and Durham, enabling fresh farm produce to be transported rapidly into the city markets. Similarly, cattle and sheep were moved quickly from many of the country markets, such as that at Rothbury, into the city slaughterhouses. The cross-country route between Newcastle and Carlisle, and that between Barnard Castle and Tebay and Penrith, enabled easy east and west access for both the raw materials of the steel industry in Cumbria and Durham, and produce such as that from the expanding dairy industry in the Eden Valley and the surrounding area.

The forward-thinking and innovative North Eastern Railway had opened a highly successful and intensively used suburban electric railway system around Newcastle-on-Tyne in 1904. This used as power, 600 volt direct current delivered by third rail. A further section of line to South Shields, south of the River Tyne, was electrified in 1938 by the LNER. This electric service ceased in January 1963 when British Railways substituted DMUs for the electric trains. The electric services north of the River Tyne were discontinued in June 1967, when they were also replaced by DMUs.

The original rolling stock was of the clerestory roof style, and was built between 1904 and 1915 at York by the NER with electrical equipment supplied by the British Thomson-Houston Co. After a disastrous fire at Heaton Car sheds in August 1918 had destroyed a large number of electric trains, a new car shed was built at South Gosforth and opened in 1923. Meanwhile, replacement stock, of a non-clerestory roof style, was built by Metro-Cammell, and delivered between 1920 and 1923. In 1937, 64 new articulated twin units were delivered from Metro-Cammell, and during 1954/5, 15 new two-car units were supplied by the British Railway works at Eastleigh to work on the South Shields route. These units were returned to the Southern Region in 1963 when the South Shields route became DMU worked.

The main towns and cities in Northumberland and Durham were served by the express passenger trains on the East Coast Main Line, and Berwick, Newcastle, Durham and Darlington all had fast and semi-fast passenger trains serving Edinburgh, Leeds and London. From 1948, the Peppercorn class A1 and A2 Pacifics joined the Gresley class A4 and A3 Pacifics in handling all the fast passenger traffic on this route. It was not until 1960 and 1961, with the introduction of the English Electric type 4 and type 5 diesel electric locomotives allocated to Haymarket in Edinburgh, Gateshead and Finsbury Park in London, that these Pacifics were gradually replaced and moved to lesser duties and minor routes, or sent to the scrapyard. DMUs also began appearing on many branch line services around Newcastle and Darlington from 1957, and it was only in the industrial heartlands of Durham and Northumberland that main line steam traction remained in use until the final locomotive allocations were withdrawn from Sunderland and West Hartlepool depots in September 1967.

January 1948 to December 1950

From Nationalisation to the eve of the introduction of the BR Standard steam locomotives

The Counties of Northumberland and Durham fell within the North Eastern Region of British Railways, which came into being with the Nationalisation of the railways in January 1948. The role of the new British Railways was to restore the railways to pre-war standards, and it became the owner of a large number of locomotives. BR acquired in the region of 1,100 ex-NER designed locomotives, almost 350 of which were 0-6-0 tender classes such as J21, J24, J25, J26 and J27. These, together with over 100 class G5 0-4-4 tank locomotives, handled the majority of the passenger and goods traffic on the many branches and secondary lines throughout the two counties. Heavy goods traffic, such as the massive amounts of coal and minerals, were handled by over 200 examples of the powerful class Q5, Q6 and Q7 0-8-0s.

During LNER days, many new types of locomotives were designed and introduced for East Coast Main line duties, such as classes A4, A3, A2, B1 and V2 for fast passenger and goods trains. These classes continued to work those types of traffic in BR days, and indeed many survived right up to the end of steam operation within the two counties. Class V1 and V3 2-6-2 tanks were introduced to replace many of the pre-grouping tanks such as the ageing class A5 and A8 on suburban and cross-country passenger work, and class J39 0-6-0 mixed traffic locomotives were introduced for goods and secondary passenger trains. From 1948 onwards, BR started to take delivery of several classes of locomotive designed by the LNER towards the end of its existence. These included class L1 2-6-4 tanks, class K1 2-6-0s and of course the powerful, Peppercorn class A1 and A2 Pacifics. These found homes at depots in the Eastern, North Eastern and Scottish Regions from Kings Cross to York, Gateshead and Haymarket.

Early in 1948, Mr RA Riddles, responsible for mechanical and electrical engineering, organised a committee to make recommendations concerning the standardisation of locomotive parts, and the selection of the best of existing locomotive types that would form the basis for a future construction programme. The main criteria for new locomotives were that they should be cheap to build, economical to work, easy to service and repair, offer improved driving and firing conditions for crews, and have a route availability that would enable them to work virtually anywhere on the system.

The result was a list of 12 types ranging initially from a class 7 Pacific to a class 2 2-6-2 tank with provision later for a heavy freight locomotive. All 12 types were to be built with 2 cylinders fitted with Walschaerts valve gear, self-cleaning smokeboxes, rocking grates and self-emptying ash pans.

Meanwhile, class J21 and J25 0-6-0s were the mainstay of traffic over Stainmore between Barnard Castle and Penrith and Tebay with class G5 0-4-4 and class A8 4-6-2 tanks handling much of the passenger traffic on the many branch lines, such as that to Rothbury, and the Sunderland to Durham services. Heavy goods traffic such as the coal trains between collieries, ports and power stations, were handled by class Q6 and Q7 0-8-0 and class J27 0-6-0 locomotives. Immediately after the end of the Second World War, a large number of ex-WD "Austerity" 2-8-0 locomotives were allocated to depots in Northumberland and Durham, and these could be seen sharing this heavy work with J27, Q6 and Q7 class locomotives.

The NCB had similarly acquired large numbers of veteran steam locomotives with some being pre-grouping types, examples of NER designs being found at several colliery complexes in the two counties. Locomotives purpose-built for pre-NCB colliery owners included examples from Andrew Barclay, Fowler, Hunslet, Kitson & Co and Robert Stephenson, to name only a few. Seaham Harbour also owned a stable of ageing steam locomotives to service the busy coal staithes there. Again, examples of NER-designed locomotives could be found working here bringing coal from nearby collieries.

Wednesday 28th July 1948. This splendid view of Newcastle Central station was taken from the top of the castle. Ex-LNER class A4 4-6-2 No 60012 *Commonwealth of Australia*, still in garter blue livery, is seen passing non-stop through the station at the head of the down Flying Scotsman. Built at Doncaster works in 1937, this locomotive would be allocated to Haymarket depot in Edinburgh for virtually its entire working life. It was moved to Ferryhill in Aberdeen in the early 1960s to assist with the fast three-hour expresses then timetabled between Glasgow and Aberdeen. Withdrawal would follow in 1964. *(KC Footer)*

Right: Tuesday 14th September 1948. At Hartley Main Colliery, Seaton Delaval, 0-6-0 locomotive No 6 looks in good condition. Built by Robert Stephenson & Co in 1899, this locomotive had originally been sold to the Seaton Delaval Coal Company, and there numbered 9. It was acquired by the Hartley Main Collieries in 1929 and renumbered 6. *(ACJ Ball)*

Opposite page: April 1948. In sparkling condition and only eight months old, ex-LNER class B1 4-6-0 No 1217 is still proudly wearing her LNER livery and identity. Having been delivered from the North British Locomotive Co (NBL) Queens Park Works, Glasgow in August the previous year, she is seen here at Carlisle waiting to depart with the 2.00pm train for Newcastle. The front bufferbeam clearly shows that she was allocated to Carlisle. She would be withdrawn from service during 1962. *(RF Roberts)*

Tuesday 14th September 1948. At Wrekenton Bank Top, the unmistakable lines of ex-NER class H (LNER class Y7) 0-4-0 tank are discernible, albeit with a reduced-height chimney. No 1308 (her LNER number) is looking in sad condition. Built at Gateshead works in 1891, she was sold to Pelaw Main Collieries in 1931, and withdrawn in 1963 having served 72 years in total. *(ACJ Ball)*

Tuesday 14th September 1948. At Whitburn Colliery, previously part of the South Shields, Whitburn and Marsden Group, we see their No 6, which is actually ex-NER class C (LNER class J21) 0-6-0 No 1509. Built originally at Gateshead works in 1889 as a 2-cylinder compound, she was later converted to a 2-cylinder simple, and sold to the Harton Coal Company in 1935; she would be withdrawn in 1951. *(ACJ Ball)*

Wednesday 15ᵗʰ September 1948. Three years after the end of World War II, the Seaham Harbour and Dock Company, approximately six miles south of Sunderland, was still shipping over one million tons of coal a year from the forest of timber and concrete staithes in its moderately-sized harbour. To service the facility, the company owned a fleet of ageing steam locomotives, including this strange looking and veteran 0-4-0VBT No 17, built by Head Wrightson of Thornaby-on-Tees in 1873. At the end of its working life in 1962, having served for 89 years, it became a static exhibit, and has since been moved to the North of England Open Air Museum at Beamish. *(ACJ Ball)*

Wednesday 15th September 1948. At South Hetton Colliery, 0-6-0 saddle tank No 9 *Sir George* is seen shunting wagons – note the extra-large dumb buffers. The origins of this locomotive seem to have become blurred by time. It might have originally been a LNWR 0-6-0 tank built in the 1840s, and rebuilt as a saddle tank before being sold to the Alexandra Docks Railway towards the end of the 19ᵗʰ century. It was sold to South Hetton Colliery in 1900, and appears to have been withdrawn in 1953. *(ACJ Ball)*

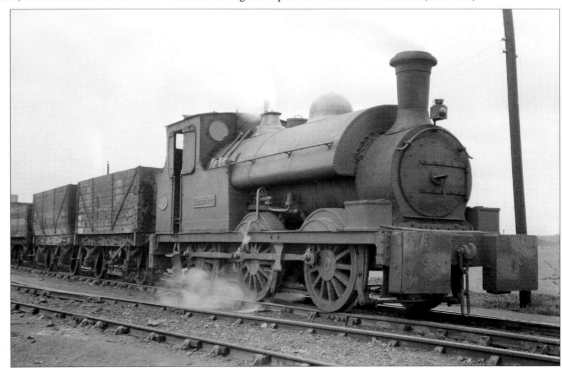

Wednesday 15th September 1948. At Hetton-le-Hole, Lambton Hetton & Joicey Collieries Ltd (LH&JC) 0-6-0 tank No 41 simmers between duties. She was built by Kitson & Co in 1917, and appears to have been acquired from the ROD after the First World War. She would be withdrawn late in 1964. *(ACJ Ball)*

Wednesday 15th September 1948. At the Philadelphia engine shed of the LH&JC system, 0-6-0 No 4 sits out of steam outside the shed. Built by Black Hawthorn in 1866, it appears to have been out of service by 1954. *(ACJ Ball)*

Wednesday 15th September 1948. Again at the Philadelphia engine shed of the LH&JC system, 0-6-0 No 9 is also out of steam. Built in 1877 at the Lambton works at Philadelphia, it continued working until 1965. *(ACJ Ball)*

Wednesday 15th September 1948. Sitting outside the LH&JC engine shed at Philadelphia, 0-6-0 tank No 27 is also out of steam. This veteran locomotive started life as a 2-4-0 built by Robert Stephenson in 1845 for the North Eastern Railway. She was sold to the LH&JC system in 1898, and rebuilt by them in the form we see here. She would be withdrawn in 1968. *(ACJ Ball)*

Wednesday 15th September 1948. Waiting to leave Philadelphia with a full head of steam is LH&JC 0-6-0 No 1, which was built by Hudswell, Clarke and Rodgers in 1866. Note the unusual outside frames of this locomotive, which appears to have been withdrawn from service in 1954. *(ACJ Ball)*

Thursday 16th September 1948. At Barnard Castle station, ex-NER class C (LNER class J21) 0-6-0 No E5098 has just arrived with the 4.10pm train from Darlington. The photographer had travelled on the train, and noted that it departed from Darlington half a minute late, arriving at Barnard Castle half a minute later than its scheduled arrival time of 4.50pm. The locomotive was one of the Darlington works built examples of the class constructed in 1891 as a 2-cylinder compound, which was later rebuilt as a 2-cylinder simple. She would be withdrawn in 1954 numbered 65098. *(ACJ Ball)*

Friday 17th September 1948. At Darlington locomotive depot, ex-NER class 290 (LNER class J77) 0-6-0 tank No 68423 shows of its new British Railways identity. A true veteran, this locomotive was originally built at Gateshead works as an 0-4-4 well tank, later to be rebuilt as an 0-6-0 tank, and finally withdrawn towards the end of 1957 having seen 79 years of service. *(ACJ Ball)*

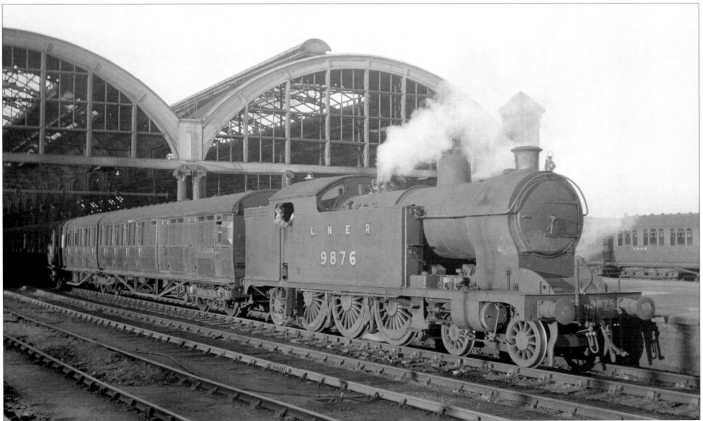

Friday 17th September 1948. Waiting to leave Darlington station with a stopping train, which includes a Gresley Articulated Twin, is ex-LNER class A8 4-6-2 tank no 9876, still wearing its LNER identity. Originally built by the NER at Darlington works in 1920 as a 3-cylinder class D (LNER class H1) 4-4-4 tank locomotive to a design by Vincent Raven, she was rebuilt by the LNER in 1934 as a 4-6-2 tank and designated class A8. This example would be withdrawn in 1957 numbered 69876. *(ACJ Ball)*

August 1949. Departing from Penrith with a "stopper" to Kirkby Stephen is ex-NER class C (LNER class J21) 0-6-0 No 65040. Built at Gateshead works in 1889 as a 2-cylinder compound locomotive, it would later be converted to a 2-cylinder simple and be withdrawn in 1952.
(PB Whitehouse)

Tuesday 27th September 1949. In good clean condition, 0-4-0 saddle tank No 22 pauses between shunting duties at the Philadelphia Colliery. Built in 1881 by Hudswell Clarke, she would survive until scrapped in 1958 having given 77 years of service. *(WA Camwell)*

Tuesday 27ᵗʰ September 1949. This Robert Stephenson and Hawthorn 0-6-0 saddle tank is brand new having arrived at the Philadelphia Colliery earlier in the year. Numbered 2 in the NCB No 2 Area she would be scrapped as late as 1970. *(WA Camwell)*

Sunday 1ˢᵗ January 1950. On this New Years Day at Blaydon shed, ex-NER class T2 (LNER class Q6) 0-8-0 No 63381 sits in a line of locomotives on this apparently quiet day. Built in 1917 at Darlington works, she would survive a further 16 years to be withdrawn in 1966. *(BKB Green)*

May 1950. With its single coach train, ex-NER class C (LNER class J21) 0-6-0 No 65119 is seen arriving at Tebay with a service from Kirkby Stephen. Built at Gateshead works in 1894, she would be withdrawn 60 years later in 1954. *(RF Roberts)*

May 1950. Smartly turned out, as always, ex-NER class E1 (LNER class J72) 0-6-0 tank No 68680 sports LNER livery, but British Railways identity, whilst working as one of the Newcastle Central station pilots. Built to a Wilson Worsdell design in 1899 at Darlington works, she would be withdrawn in 1961 having served 62 years. *(RF Roberts)*

Monday 8th May 1950. Ex-LNER class J39 0-6-0 No 64705 is waiting to depart Reedsmouth station with a Hexham to Riccarton Junction train. One of the first of the class to be constructed at Darlington works in 1926, she would give 36 years service before being withdrawn in 1962. The Border Counties Railway opened the route between Hexham and Riccarton Junction in 1862. Operated by the NBR from the outset, the passenger service was withdrawn in October 1956, with the whole line closing to all traffic in November 1963. *(Ian Allan Library)*

Friday 26th May 1950. Reputed to be the highest market town in England, Alston was reached by a branch of the NER Newcastle–Carlisle route from a junction at Haltwhistle. Seen here is ex-NER class O (LNER class G5) 0-4-4 tank No 67315 approaching Alston station with the 2-coach 3.30pm departure from Haltwhistle. Based on a design of 1894, the locomotive was constructed at Darlington works in 1900 and would be withdrawn in 1958. Note the snowplough in the left background of the photograph. *(R Hewitt)*

Tuesday 30th May 1950. Ex-NER class C (LNER class J21) 0-6-0 No 65047 hurries along the West Coast Main Line at Yanwath, just south of Penrith, with a Darlington-bound "stopper". Built at Gateshead works in 1889 as a 2-cylinder compound, she was rebuilt later as a 2-cylinder simple. She would survive a further four years being withdrawn from service at the end of 1954. *(R Hewitt)*

Friday 16th June 1950. Another photograph, taken at Darlington, of ex-NER class C1 (LNER class J21) 0-6-0 No 65119 clearly shows the graceful lines of the class. This example was one of a class built at Gateshead works in 1894 as a 2-cylinder simple locomotive as opposed to the bulk of the class, which were built as 2-cylinder compounds and later converted to 2-cylinder simple. *(ED Bruton)*

Friday 16th June 1950. The well-balanced lines of ex-LNER 3-cylinder class V1 2-6-2 tank No 67665 are clear here, with the locomotive bearing its new identity and livery. Built at Doncaster works in 1938, she would be withdrawn in 1961. Photographed at Darlington, possibly after an overhaul, she was at this time allocated to Kipps depot in Glasgow. *(ED Bruton)*

Saturday 24th June 1950. At Darlington works, ex-NER class S3 (LNER class B16/1) 4-6-0 No 61478 has just had a new boiler fitted, and is looking very smart in its new ex-works BR livery. Built to a Vincent Raven design at the same works in 1920 as one of a class of mixed traffic locomotives, she would give a further ten years service before being withdrawn late in 1960. *(HC Casserley)*

Saturday 24th June 1950. This EMU train waits to depart Newcastle Central station with a stopping service to South Shields. These units were part of the order built by Metro-Cammell in 1920/21, and rebuilt in 1937/38 to replace the original NER stock lost in the fire of August 1918. *(HC Casserley)*

Sunday 25th June 1950. Sitting inside Gateshead depot, and bearing a 52A shed code, is ex-LNER class Y1/2 4-wheeled, Sentinel-built locomotive No 68141. Purchased by the LNER in 1929 from the Sentinel Co, she was finally allocated to Gateshead depot in 1947 from where she would be withdrawn in 1952. *(HC Casserley)*

Sunday 25th June 1950. At Tyne Dock depot, ex-NER class T3 (LNER class Q7) 0-8-0 No 63471 waits its next duty. This powerful locomotive was constructed at Darlington works in 1924 as part of a second batch of ten locomotives in the class, the first batch of five locomotives having been constructed during 1919. The whole class totalling 15 locomotives was withdrawn towards the end of 1962. *(HC Casserley)*

Sunday 25th June 1950. The powerful presence of ex-NER class P3 (LNER class J27) 0-6-0 No 65869 is clearly apparent in this photograph taken at Heaton depot. Built at Darlington works in 1922, she would survive until almost the end of steam locomotive allocations in the North East, being withdrawn early in 1967. *(HC Casserley)*

Sunday 25th June 1950. Another photograph taken at Heaton depot, this time showing ex-NER class B (LNER class N8) 0-6-2 tank No 69372 sporting its new British Railways identity. Another veteran, she was built at Darlington works in 1886 as a 2-cylinder compound later converted to a 2-cylinder simple. She would survive a few more months to be withdrawn late in 1950 having served for 64 years. *(Ian Allan Library)*

Thursday 13th July 1950. With a spectacular signal gantry in the background at Newcastle Central station, ex-NBR "Superheated Scott" class (LNER class D30) 4-4-0 No 62422 *Caleb Balderstone* departs with the 4.30pm passenger train to Hawick. This will run to Hexham, and then traverse the former Border Counties Railway route via Reedsmouth and Riccarton Junction to arrive at Hawick at about 7.00pm. Constructed at Cowlairs works in Glasgow in 1914, the locomotive would be withdrawn in 1958. *(Ian Allan Library)*

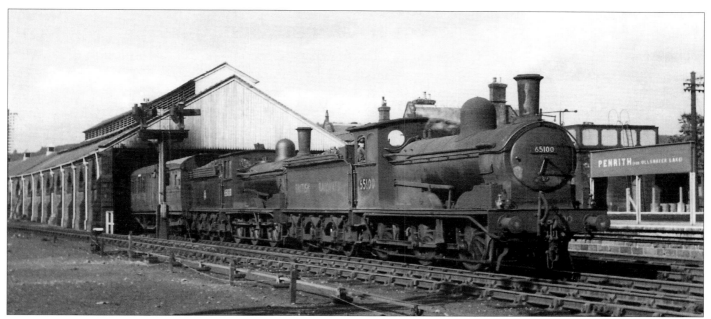

Sunday 13th August 1950. At Penrith (for Ullswater Lake) station, ex-NER class C (LNER class J21) 0-6-0 No 65100 is seen piloting classmate No 65038 with a passenger train for Darlington. Carrying express passenger train lamps and fitted with a slip coupling, No 65100 was built at Gateshead works in 1891 as a 2-cylinder compound locomotive, which was later rebuilt as a 2-cylinder simple, she would be withdrawn in 1954. No 65038 was also built at Gateshead works as a 2-cylinder compound in 1889, and would also be rebuilt as a 2-cylinder simple, similarly to be withdrawn in 1954. *(N Fields)*

Wednesday 11th October 1950. Hump shunting in No 1 up yard at Newport, Middlesbrough is ex-NER class X (LNER class T1) 4-8-0 tank No 69910. The first of this powerful 3-cylinder class to be built at Gateshead works in 1909, she was withdrawn in 1959. *(Ian Allan Library)*

January 1951 to December 1956

From the introduction of BR Standard steam locomotives to the eve of the introduction of DMUs and main-line diesel locomotives

The first of BR's new Standard locomotive types appeared in January 1951 when, amid much publicity, No 70000 *Britannia* was rolled out of Crewe works.

Unlike other regions of British Railways, the Standard locomotive classes were slow in arriving at depots in Northumberland and Durham, and initially a few Ivatt-designed class 2MT and 4MT 2-6-0s started to replace some pre-grouping locomotives such as J25 0-6-0 and G5 0-4-4 tanks. It was early in 1953 before Standard class 4 2-6-0s were being delivered to West Auckland and Sunderland depots, and they were followed a year later by examples of the Standard class 2 and class 3 2-6-0s also being allocated to West Auckland depot. These locomotives quickly became the regular workhorses over the Stainmore route, working in pairs on both passenger and goods traffic. The ending of passenger services on many branch lines in the early 1950s also saw the demise of numerous class G5 0-4-4 tanks, but whilst goods services continued on these lines, it was mostly the class J21 and J27 0-6-0s that supplied the motive power.

Toward the end of 1948, the Railway Executive had formed a committee to compare the relative merits of steam, diesel and electric motive power. This committee did not report until 1951, but in the meantime, a working party was formed to evaluate the use of lightweight diesel trains. The conclusion of the investigation was outlined in yet another report in March 1952, which led to the introduction of these lightweight diesel trains known as diesel multiple-units (DMUs).

In December 1954, the British Transport Commission published its plan for the *Modernisation and Re-equipment of British Railways.* In locomotive terms this predicted the end of steam power by announcing that no new steam locomotives would be build after the end of the 1956 programme. A Pilot Scheme was devised whereby 174 main-line diesel locomotives would be purchased, from various manufacturers, and then subjected to rigorous testing before further orders were placed. In all, 160 of these locomotives would be built with electric transmission, and they would range from an 800hp type A (later type 1) for goods work to a 2,300hp type C (type 4) for express passenger trains. In practice, many orders were placed for large numbers of

locomotives without any prolonged testing, with the result that some designs with inherent problems were produced, and consequently had short lives.

While work on building diesel locomotives was progressing, steam traction still ruled supreme with services on the East Coast Main Line being powered by class A4, A3, A2 and the newly-introduced class A1 Pacific locomotives based in Edinburgh, London and Gateshead. Away from the East Coast Main Line, local passenger traffic was still in the capable hands of class A5, A8, V1, V3 and L1 tanks, whilst the large amounts of coal still being produced by the collieries in the two counties was being transported to the power stations, coking plants and staithes by class J27 0-6-0s, Q6 and Q7 0-8-0s, ex-WD 8F 2-8-0s and a few ex-LMS and ex-LNER designed Moguls. Traffic on the Stainmore route was handled almost entirely by Standard class 4, 3 and 2 Moguls, with some assistance from a remaining few veteran class J21 0-6-0s.

The NCB was meanwhile tending to dispose of its older, non-standard locomotive types and concentrating on the use of Andrew Barclay built 0-4-0 and 0-6-0 tanks, together with an increasing number of "Austerity" 0-6-0 saddle tanks that were surplus to WD duties.

During 1955 and 1956, ten of the powerful class 9F 2-10-0 locomotives were allocated to Tyne Dock (52H) depot to handle the iron ore trains to Consett. They were fitted with two Westinghouse compressors to supply power to operate the doors on the iron ore wagons and replaced the elderly Q7 0-8-0 and O1 2-8-0 classes based at that depot.

Opposite page: Tuesday 5th June 1951. Working a train of full coal wagons near Kirkby Stephen, ex-NER class C (LNER class J21) 0-6-0 No 65078 shows off its graceful proportions on this bright summer day. Built at Darlington works in 1891 as a 2-cylinder compound and later converted to a 2-cylinder simple locomotive, she would survive until 1957 before being withdrawn. *(Ian Allan Library)*

Right: Friday 6th July 1951. With its one-coach train, ex-NER class O (LNER class G5) 0-4-4 tank No 67296 simmers quietly at Morpeth station as it waits to leave with the branch train to Rothbury. This locomotive was built at Darlington works in 1897, and was withdrawn in 1955. The passenger service on the ex-NBR Rothbury branch was withdrawn in September 1952, with the goods service lingering on until November 1963. *(WA Camwell)*

Below: Saturday 7th July 1951. The well-proportioned lines of ex-NER class C (LNER class J21) 0-6-0 no 65042 are seen here to advantage. At Scotsgap Junction, the locomotive and its one-coach train wait to depart with the 10.46am service to Reedsmouth. Built at Gateshead works in 1889, this locomotive was another example of this 2-cylinder compound class that would later be rebuilt as a 2-cylinder simple. The locomotive would be withdrawn in 1954. *(WA Camwell/SLS)*

Friday 13th July 1951. Ex-NBR class J (LNER class D30) 4-4-0 No 62422 *Caleb Balderstone* is seen here leaving Hexham with a Newcastle to Hawick train. Built in 1924 at Cowlairs works, this locomotive would be withdrawn in 1958. The passenger service on this ex-NBR line between Hexham and Riccarton Junction would last only a further five years before itself being withdrawn in October 1956. *(JN Westwood)*

Monday 30th July 1951. Working as station pilot at Newcastle Central station, this graceful looking locomotive is ex-NER class R (LNER class D20) 4-4-0 No 62351. Built in 1900 to a design by Wilson Worsdell, she was constructed at Gateshead works and would be withdrawn in 1954. *(AJ Walter)*

Thursday 23rd August 1951. This rather ungainly looking, but powerful, locomotive, is ex-NER class X (LNER class T1) 4-8-0 tank No 69921, which is engaged in hump shunting at Newport yard in Middlesbrough. She was built at Darlington works in 1925 as part of a batch of five ordered by the LNER. The class totalled 15 examples, with the original ten being built at Gateshead works in 1909 and 1910. She was the last of the class to survive being withdrawn in 1961. *(PH Wells)*

Saturday 26th January 1952. Seen here, highlighted by the low sun on this cold winter day amid the remains of a recent snowfall, ex-LNER class A4 4-6-2 No 60027 *Merlin* is working the down "Flying Scotsman" passing Dam Dykes signalbox near Annitsford, Northumberland. Built at Doncaster works in 1937, she would spend most of her working life based at Haymarket in Edinburgh, finally being allocated to Ferryhill in Aberdeen from where she would be withdrawn in 1965. *(JD Smith)*

Friday 1st February 1952. This bright winter day sees ex-NER class P1 (LNER class J25) 0-6-0 No 65673, fitted with a small snowplough, in Tebay yard having worked a goods train from Kirkby Stephen. Built in 1899 to a design by Wilson Worsdell introduced in 1898, she would give 59 years of service before being withdrawn in 1958. *(JE Wilkinson)*

Thursday 17th April 1952. This busy scene at Darlington station shows class L1 2-6-4 tank No 67754 departing with the 5.48pm train to Richmond. Meanwhile a much older design of tank locomotive, ex-GCR class 9N (LNER class A5/2) 4-6-2 tank No 69840 waits for its next duty. The A5 tank was built by Hawthorn Leslie &Co in 1926 and would be withdrawn in 1958, whilst the L1 tank was built by the NBL in 1948 and would be withdrawn after only 14 years service in 1962. *(GH Hunt)*

Saturday 17th May 1952. This excellent photograph shows ex-NER class P2 (LNER class J26) 0-6-0 No 65743 working a short local-trip goods train whilst passing Newport Yard. Constructed to a design by Wilson Worsdell, and introduced in 1904, this locomotive was built in the same year at Darlington works and would be withdrawn in 1962. *(RE Vincent)*

Friday 30th May 1952. This Wilson Worsdell designed ex-NER class P1 (LNER class J25) 0-6-0 No 65695 is working a mixed goods train westward near Gaisgill on the Kirkby Stephen to Tebay route. Based at Kirkby Stephen (51H) depot, this locomotive was built in 1900 at Gateshead works and would be withdrawn after 62 years service in 1962. *(ED Bruton)*

Friday 30th May 1952. In contrast to the older locomotive in the above photograph, we see here a modern (barely nine-month old) Ivatt designed class 2 2-6-0 No 46471 drifting down the bank from Gaisgill towards Tebay with a goods train from Darlington. Of post-nationalisation construction at Darlington works in 1951, she would be withdrawn only 11 years later in 1962. *(ED Bruton)*

Tuesday 3rd June 1952. With a heavy goods train in tow, ex-LNER class B1 4-6-0 No 61061 is seen near Chester-le-Street. Bearing an Aberdeen, Kittybrewster (61A) shed code, but having St Margaret's, Edinburgh clearly painted on the front buffer beam, the locomotive is a long way from whichever home claims her. Built by the NBL in 1946, she would survive until 1965 before being withdrawn. *(Sidney E Teasdale)*

Friday 6th June 1952. With an exceedingly interesting mixed rake of five coaches in tow, Ivatt designed class 2 2-6-0 No 46471 departs Tebay station with the 8.42am Ulverston to Durham miners special. This was one of the examples of the class built during BR days at Darlington works in 1951, so was still relatively new when this photograph was taken. *(ED Bruton)*

Friday 13th June 1952. Leaving Stockton South Yard with a train carrying coke is ex-WD 9F 2-10-0 No 90763. Built by the NBL in 1945, and numbered 73787 by the WD, she was acquired by BR in 1949/50 and appears to have spent most of her BR working life based at Carlisle Kingmoor. She would be withdrawn at the end of 1962. *(Ian Allan Library)*

Saturday 23rd August 1952. At Barnard Castle, ex-NER class C (LNER class J21) 0-6-0 No 65103 is seen leaving for Darlington with a train from Blackpool. Bearing a Darlington (51A) shed code, this veteran locomotive was built at Gateshead works in 1892 as a 2-cylinder compound, and later rebuilt as a 2-cylinder simple. She would be withdrawn in 1958. *(JW Armstrong)*

Saturday 23rd August 1952. Ex-NER class C (LNER class J21) 0-6-0 No 65040 pilots an unidentified classmate with a Kirkby Stephen to West Auckland goods train on the climb out of Barnard Castle at Coal Road signalbox. 65040 was built at Gateshead works in 1889 as a 2-cylinder compound, and later converted to a 2-cylinder simple. She would be withdrawn a month after this photograph was taken. This veteran class of locomotives was soon to be replaced by the new BR Standard class 2 2-6-0s on the cross Pennine route. *(JW Armstrong)*

Monday 8th September 1952. Looking in very clean condition for a National Coal Board locomotive, 0-6-2 tank No 10 passes Fawcett Street Junction with a Penshaw to South Dock coal train. Built by Robert Stephenson in 1909 for the LH&JC system, she would survive a further 17 years until withdrawal in 1965. *(GM Staddon/N Stead Collection)*

Saturday 13th September 1952. With the motto "Heather Belle good old pal" chalked on the smokebox door, ex-NER class C (LNER class J21) 0-6-0 No 65035 is seen shunting a goods train in the station yard at Rothbury. Built at Gateshead works in 1889 as a 2-cylinder compound, she would later be converted to a 2-cylinder simple and be withdrawn in 1956 after 67 years of service. This was the last day of passenger services on the branch. *(JW Armstrong)*

Saturday 25th October 1952. At the eastern end of Barnard Castle station, Ivatt designed class 2 2-6-0 No 46476 heads a goods train for Darlington under the splendid signal gantry bearing an array of lower quadrant signals. The locomotive was one of the BR Darlington built batch in 1951, and she would be withdrawn in 1962. *(JW Armstrong)*

Saturday 8th November 1952. On this dull November day, LNER class A5/2 4-6-2 tank No 69835 is preparing to depart Spennymoor station with a passenger train. Designed by Robinson for the GCR as a class 9N, and primarily built for suburban traffic out of Marylebone in London, this example was built by Hawthorn Leslie & Co for the LNER in 1925, and would be withdrawn in 1958. *(JW Armstrong)*

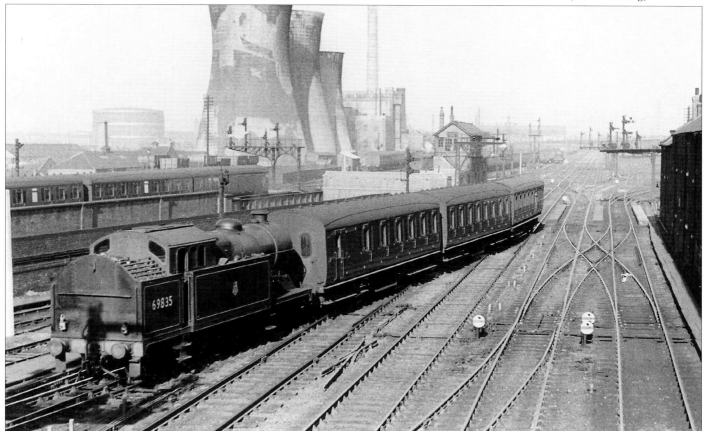

Sunday 22nd February 1953. Three months later, and looking north from the footbridge at Darlington station, the same locomotive, No 69835, is seen arriving with a train from Ferryhill. *(Ian Allan Library)*

Above: April 1953. Built primarily for semi-fast passenger services, the North Eastern Railway class D 4-4-4 tanks were powerful 3-cylinder locomotives, which were re-classified Class H1 by the LNER after the grouping. Seen here having arrived at Sunderland station with a "stopper" from Newcastle is No 69853. Built at Darlington works in 1913 as a 4-4-4 tank, she would be rebuilt by the LNER in 1935 as a 4-6-2 tank, the class being designated A8. Surprisingly she would survive until 1960 before being withdrawn. *(P. Ransome-Wallis)*

Left: Wednesday 24th June 1953. Filling the sky over Newcastle Central station with a blanket of smoke and steam, ex-NER class B (LNER class N8) 0-6-2 tank No 69390 is seen attempting to move a heavy train of empty coaching stock. Looking well cared for, this locomotive was built in 1889 at Darlington works as a 2-cylinder compound, and later converted to a 2-cylinder simple. She would be the last example of the class to be withdrawn late in 1956. *(KW Wightman)*

Above: Friday 26th June 1953. On the penultimate day of passenger services on the Wearhead branch, ex-NER class C (LNER class J21) 0-6-0 No 65061 draws into Stanhope station with a four-coach train with two prospective passengers on the platform. This locomotive, allocated to West Auckland (51F) depot, was built at Gateshead works in 1890, and would be withdrawn in 1958. *(AB Crompton)*

Right: Sunday 9th May 1954. Often to be seen working passenger trains, the ex-LNER class J39 0-6-0s were designed as mixed traffic locomotives. Here we see No 64916, allocated to West Hartlepool (51C) depot, working a Middlesbrough to Newcastle passenger train whilst climbing the 1 in 50 gradient to Hesleden on the Wellfield Junction line, which was normally closed to passenger traffic. This class of locomotive, classified 4P5F by British Railways, was designed by Sir Nigel Gresley, and introduced in 1926. Built by Beyer Peacock in 1936, this locomotive would be withdrawn in 1961. *(O Metcalfe)*

Above: Monday 17th May 1954. Simmering quietly between duties at Tyne Dock depot is ex-LNER class O1 2-8-0 No 63760. Originally built to a design by Robinson in 1918 as a class O4, she would be rebuilt by Thompson in 1946 as a class O1. She is fitted with two Westinghouse air pumps to facilitate working the doors on the iron ore wagons working between Tyne Dock and Consett. *(AG Ellis)*

Left: Friday 11th June 1954. At West Hartlepool goods depot, ex-NER class E1 (LNER class J72) 0-6-0 tank No 68711 sits quietly outside the depot awaiting its next duty. Built at Darlington works in 1920, she would be withdrawn in 1961. *(GM Staddon/N Stead Collection)*

Above: Saturday 3rd July 1954. Station pilot at Darlington station on this day was class J72 0-6-0 tank No 69022. Based on an unaltered design of 1898, this locomotive is deceptively only three years old, having been built at Darlington works in 1951. She would be withdrawn only 11 years later in 1962. *(Martin A Cooper)*

Right: Saturday 3rd July 1954. At Darlington station, a pair of LNER class A8 4-6-2 tanks pose for the camera. On the left is No 69873, allocated to Middlesbrough (51D) depot, and on the right, No 69894 allocated to Saltburn (51K) depot. Both locomotives were built originally at Darlington works as class D (LNER class H1) 4-4-4 tanks, the former in 1920, and the latter in 1922. Locomotives in this class were rebuilt as 4-6-2s in the 1930s, and designated class A8 by the LNER. Both locomotives would be withdrawn during 1960. *(Martin A Cooper)*

Saturday 17th July 1954. This Durham Miners Gala Day sees BR Standard class 2 2-6-0 No 78015 working a Durham to Bishop Auckland special near Relly Mill Junction, Durham. Built at Darlington works earlier in 1954, this locomotive would only survive nine years before being withdrawn in 1963. *(JW Armstrong)*

Sunday 25th July 1954. Standing behind Penrith No 2 signalbox, ex-NER class C (LNER class J21) 0-6-0 No 65091, allocated to West Auckland (51F) depot, simmers prior to working a train to Kirkby Stephen. Built at Gateshead works in 1891, this locomotive was one of the class constructed as a 2-cylinder compound that was later converted to a 2-cylinder simple. She would be withdrawn in 1957. *(TK Widd)*

Above: Tuesday 3rd August 1954. Looking well cared for by the staff at Darlington (51A) depot, ex-NER class C (LNER class J21) 0-6-0 No 65103 is seen here departing from Kirkby Stephen East station with the 10.32am Penrith to Darlington service. This locomotive was built at Gateshead works in 1892, and would be withdrawn in 1958. *(JE Wilkinson)*

Left: Tuesday 17th August 1954. Working hard with a heavy eastbound passenger train approaching Stainmore Summit, BR Standard class 3 2-6-0 No 77003 pilots an unidentified classmate. Only six months old, and recently delivered from Swindon works, 77003 was allocated to West Auckland (51F) depot and is already looking uncared for. She would be withdrawn 12 years later. *(JW Armstrong)*

Above: Tuesday 17th August 1954. At Bleath Gill cutting east of Barras, BR Standard class 3 2-6-0 No 77013 is only two months old having been constructed at Swindon works, and delivered to Darlington depot. Seen here working a Penrith to Darlington train, she would be withdrawn in 1966. *(JW Armstrong)*

Left: Tuesday 24th August 1954. The Haltwhistle to Alston branch traffic was regularly worked by ex-LNER class J39 0-6-0s, and here we see No 64814 pausing between duties at Alston. Classified 4P5F by British Railways, these locomotives were to be seen working over most of the Eastern and North Eastern Regions of British Railways. Built in Darlington works at 1930, this locomotive would be withdrawn in 1962. *(RF Roberts)*

Right: Wednesday 8th September 1954. Making a splendid display whilst departing Darlington station, ex-LNER class A3 4-6-2 No 60081 *Shotover*, is working the down "North Briton". Built by the NBL Hyde Park Works in 1924 as a class A1, she would be rebuilt as an A3 in 1928 and withdrawn in 1962. *(RK Evans)*

Below: Friday 10th September 1954. This Penshaw to South Dock NCB coal train is seen at Millfield being hauled by ex-LH&JC 0-6-2 tank No 31. Built by Kitson & Co in 1907, she would survive in service until 1968.
(Staddon/Stead Collection)

Saturday 11th December 1954. BR Standard class 3 2-6-2 tank No 82027 is seen departing Barnard Castle, and passing the East signalbox with the 10.32am train from Penrith to Darlington. Built at Swindon earlier in 1954, and originally intended for use on the Western Region, this locomotive was allocated to Kirkby Stephen depot. She would be withdrawn only 12 years later in 1966. *(JW Armstrong)*

February 1955. The exhaust from ex-LNER class A2/1 4-6-2 No 60507 *Highland Chieftain* is splendidly highlighted on this cold winter day as she hurries by with a down fitted goods train near Cramlington. Built at Darlington works in 1944, she was one of four examples designed by Edward Thompson utilising a class V2 boiler. She would be withdrawn in 1960. *(JD Smith)*

Sunday 24th April 1955. This graceful looking locomotive is ex-NER class R (LNER class D20) 4-4-0 No 62383. Constructed to a Wilson Worsdell design at Gateshead works in 1907, she would be withdrawn from service almost exactly 50 years later in 1957. She is seen here looking in excellent external condition at Darlington depot. *(TK Widd)*

Monday 12th September 1955. Waiting to depart Newcastle Central station with the 12.37pm train to Bristol is ex-LNER class V2 2-6-2 No 60835 *The Green Howard, Alexandra, Princess of Wales's own Yorkshire Regiment*. Built at Darlington works in 1938, this locomotive would be withdrawn in 1965. *(RF Roberts)*

Above: Wednesday 14th September 1955. Newly delivered from Eastleigh works earlier in the year, this EMU (leading car No E77114) is departing Newcastle Central station with the 9.42am stopping service to South Shields. This stock, which was used on the South Shields services, would be transferred to the Southern Region when this electric service was discontinued in 1963.

Below: Wednesday 14th September 1955. This photograph shows one of the replacement Motor Parcels Vans built by Metro-Cammell in 1921 for the electric suburban system in Newcastle. No E29493E was rebuilt in 1938, and withdrawn from service in 1956. She is seen here at Newcastle Central station with ex-NER class R (LNER class D20) 4-4-0 No 62383 in the background. *(Both RF Roberts)*

Right: Saturday 9th June 1956. Waiting for the starter to come off at Reedsmouth station, ex-LNER class D49/2 4-4-0 No 62771 *The Rufford* is seen at the head of the 4.27pm Newcastle to Hawick train. This route would be closed to passenger traffic in October of the same year. This 3-cylinder locomotive was built at Darlington works in 1935, one of the batch fitted with Lentz rotary cam poppet valves, and she would survive to be withdrawn two years later in 1958. *(IS Carr)*

Below: Saturday 16th June 1956. Arriving at Tebay with the 9.40am service from Newcastle to Blackpool are BR Standard class 3 2-6-0 Nos 77003 and 77002. Both locomotives were built at Swindon in 1954, and allocated to West Auckland (51F) depot. The former was withdrawn in 1966 and the latter in 1967. *(JE Wilkinson)*

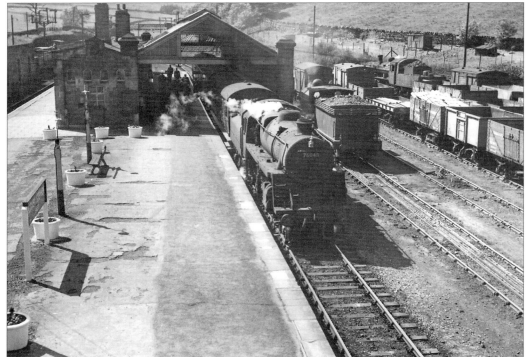

Left: Monday 25th June 1956. This bright summer day sees BR Standard class 4 2-6-0 No 76048 waiting to depart Kirkby Stephen East station with the 2.55pm Penrith to Darlington service. Built at Doncaster in 1955, she would be withdrawn in 1967. In the background in the busy goods yard can be seen an unidentified class J21 and an unidentified BR Standard class 2. *(TG Hepburn)*

Below: Saturday 14th July 1956. The old and new working together. At Tebay station, ex-NER class C (LNER class J21) 0-6-0 No 65064 is seen piloting BR Standard class 3 2-6-0 No 77004 whilst working the 7.32 am South Shields to Blackpool train. Built 64 years apart, 65064 at Gateshead works in 1890 and 77004 at Swindon works in 1954, the former would be withdrawn in 1958 and the latter in 1966. *(JE Wilkinson)*

Left: Saturday 28th July 1956. BR Standard class 4 2-6-0 Nos 76024 and 76021 are seen here departing Tebay yard with a train of empties bound for Durham. Both locomotives were constructed at Doncaster works, 76024 in 1953 and 76021 a year earlier in 1952. Both locomotives would be withdrawn in 1966. *(JE Wilkinson)*

Below: Saturday 4th August 1956. On this beautiful summer day, BR Standard class 3 2-6-0 No 77011 simmers quietly in the bay platform at Hexham station. The locomotive was built at Swindon works in 1954, and would be withdrawn in 1966. The train would leave later that afternoon to traverse the Border Counties line to Reedsmouth and Riccarton Junction. *(WS Sellar)*

Left: Tuesday 21st August 1956. Waiting at Penrith station to depart with the 10.32am train to Darlington is BR Standard class 3 2-6-2 tank No 82029. She was built at Swindon works in 1954, and allocated to Darlington (51A) depot. She would be withdrawn in 1967. *(R Leslie)*

Below: Wednesday 29th August 1956. In charge of the 2.00pm passenger train from Carlisle to Newcastle, ex-LNER class V2 2-6-2 No 60812 is seen arriving at Hexham station. Allocated to Heaton (52B) depot, this locomotive was constructed at Darlington works in 1937, and would be withdrawn in 1964. *(IS Carr)*

Saturday 1st September 1956. Near Stranton, West Hartlepool, LNER class A5/2 4-6-2 tank No 69838 is looking in good external condition as she works a southbound train. Built by Hawthorn Leslie & Co in 1925 for the LNER, the design was based on the successful Robinson 9N class. She would be withdrawn in 1958. *(GM Staddon/N Stead Collection)*

Saturday 22nd September 1956. Working an empty coaching stock train for the Bellingham Agricultural Show, ex-NER class C (LNER class J21) 0-6-0 No 65061 is seen here at Reedsmouth. Still carrying its Westinghouse air pump, and allocated to Gateshead (52A) depot, this locomotive was built at Gateshead works in 1890, and would be withdrawn in 1958. *(IS Carr)*

January 1957 to September 1967
From the introduction of DMUs and main line diesel locomotives to the end of main-line steam

Early in 1957, Diesel Multiple Units (DMUs) built by Metro-Cammell started to appear in the Newcastle area, in preparation for their introduction to services between Newcastle and Carlisle and the Alston branch in February of the same year. Further batches of Metro-Cammell units were delivered to Newcastle in 1957, and during February 1958, DMUs started to handle the passenger traffic out of Darlington over the Stainmore route to Penrith. Further units from both Metro-Cammell and BRC&W were delivered to Newcastle and Darlington during 1958 to work services to Middlesbrough and Saltburn.

The allocation of main line diesel locomotives to depots in the two counties began late in 1959 with a batch of 14 English Electric type 4s being sent to Gateshead depot for use on the ECML. So successful were these that further batches of the same type followed to the same depot throughout 1960. During 1961, the 22 examples of the powerful English Electric type 5 Deltic locomotives were being delivered to depots at Finsbury Park, Haymarket and Gateshead to replace the ageing fleet of ex-LNER Pacifics working the express passenger trains on the ECML. From the spring of 1961 until the winter of the same year, six examples of this type were delivered to Gateshead depot. The increased use of these type 4 and 5 locomotives inevitably led to many examples of class A4, A3, A2, A1, V2 and B1 steam locomotives being made redundant and sent for scrap, or moved to secondary duties.

From 1960 onwards, other successful main line diesel locomotive types were being allocated to depots within the area. BR/Sulzer type 2s were being allocated to Gateshead and Thornaby depots throughout 1960, 1961, 1962 and 1963, whilst BRC&W type 2s and English Electric type 3s were being allocated to the same depots during 1962. Somewhat surprisingly, two batches of the poor performing Clayton type 1s were allocated to both Gateshead and Thornaby during 1964, and five newly-built English Electric type 1s were allocated to Thornaby as late as the summer of 1967.

All this activity with diesel allocations led, not surprisingly, to massive withdrawals of steam traction within the two counties. By the mid-1960s, steam traction had virtually disappeared from the ECML, but it was still utilised on the many rural goods services such as those to Woodburn and Rothbury, and particularly on the coal traffic from the many collieries still operating in the two counties. For example, coal from Ashington Colliery was transported to Stella Power Station north of the river Tyne and Cambois Power Station, south of the river Tyne, received coal from Bedlington Colliery. Inevitably, as collieries in the

Northumberland and Durham coalfields ceased production and closed during the 1960s, the use of the transhipment staithes at Lambton in Sunderland ceased in January 1967. Those at Seaham Harbour survived a little longer, but when the NCB cancelled all coal shipments out of Seaham in 1978, demolition of the staithes began almost immediately.

One significant line closure that took place during this period was that of the Stainmore route. Passenger services between Barnard Castle and Penrith ceased on 22nd January 1962, with the last passenger train running on 20th January. The local communities along the route fought long and hard against this closure, but the railway authorities would not be swayed, and the line closed amid great controversy.

Not only was steam traction being withdrawn, but the highly-utilised suburban electric trains running both north and south of the River Tyne were withdrawn due to the lack of reinvestment in the infrastructure and the ageing rolling stock. Services south of the Tyne were withdrawn in January 1963, and those north of the Tyne in 1967, both to be replaced by DMUs.

With the Nationalisation of railways in January 1948, the railways in both Northumberland and Durham had been placed within the North Eastern Region of British Railways, and given a distinctive orange "corporate colour". It was with some shock that late in 1966 it was announced that from January 1967, the North Eastern Region would lose its autonomy and be merged with the Eastern Region, the headquarters of the new enlarged region to be in York. The year 1967 also saw the final run-down of main line steam traction within the two counties when in September of that year the last locomotives, mostly class J27 0-6-0s and ex-WD 8F 2-8-0s were withdrawn from Sunderland and West Hartlepool depots.

Sunday 31st March 1957. Looking to be in excellent condition, class A1 4-6-2 No 60151 *Midlothian* is seen here at speed passing Cox Green station as it heads the 1.05pm Newcastle and Sunderland to London Kings Cross train, diverted due to engineering works. Built as one of the last batch of the class at Darlington works in 1949, this Gateshead allocated locomotive would be withdrawn eight years later in 1965 having given only 16 years service. *(IS Carr)*

Sunday 12th May 1957. Another Newcastle to London Kings Cross train diverted due to engineering works. This is the 3.50pm Sundays-only hauled by ex-LNER class A4 4-6-2 No 60019 *Bittern*, seen here arriving at Eaglescliffe. Looking well cared for by the Gateshead depot staff, this locomotive was built at Doncaster works in 1937, and withdrawn from Ferryhill depot in Aberdeen in 1966. She was purchased privately, and went on to operate many main line specials before being dismantled for a major overhaul, returning to main line service in 2008. *(BKB Green)*

Opposite page: Sunday 10th February 1957. Approaching the end of steam locomotive manufacturing at Darlington works, this photograph of the erecting shop shows, from left to right, Standard class 2 2-6-2 tanks Nos 84020/1/2 and 3 during construction. The order for the final ten examples of this class would be completed in June of the year when No 84029 left the works. None of the locomotives shown here survived in service for more than seven years, and none of the class would survive into the preservation scene. *(A Brown)*

Saturday 20th July 1957. On Miners Gala Day, Durham would be a very busy station with specials arriving during the morning. Looking in excellent external condition, ex-NER class S3 (LNER class B16) 4-6-0 No 61435 is seen departing Durham station at the head of the 12.12pm Scarborough to Newcastle train. Built to a 1919-introduced, Raven 3-cylinder design in 1922, she would be rebuilt in 1949 and withdrawn during 1964. Note Durham motive power depot in the background. *(A Brown)*

Wednesday 14th August 1957. Seen here at Penrith, BR Standard class 4, 2-6-0 No 76050 leads classmate No 76021 as they work light-engine towards the Darlington line. Both locomotives were allocated to West Auckland (51F) depot, and both built at Doncaster works. 76050 was delivered in 1956, and withdrawn in 1965, surviving only nine years, whilst 76021 was delivered as part of an earlier batch in 1952, and would be withdrawn in 1966. *(KS Hudson)*

Thursday 5th September 1957. In an extremely dirty condition, ex-NER class O (LNER class G5) 0-4-4 tank No 67258 waits to leave Sunderland station with the 2.08pm train to Durham. Bearing a (54A) Sunderland shed code, this locomotive was built in 1895 at Darlington works, and managed to survive a further month before being withdrawn in October 1957. *(IS Carr)*

Tuesday 1st April 1958. This vintage 0-4-0 saddle tank proudly displays its identification, NCB No 2 Area, and is No 23 based at the Philadelphia Colliery. Built by Black Hawthorn of Gateshead in 1882, she would be scrapped in 1963. *(A Brown)*

Saturday 12th April 1958. A busy scene at the Southern end of Durham station. Ex-LNER class A8 4-6-2 tanks Nos 69858 and 69850 wait patiently for their next duties in the bay platforms. 69858 was built at Darlington works as a class D 4-4-4 tank in 1913 and rebuilt as a 4-6-2 tank in 1936; she would be withdrawn during 1960. 69850, the first of the class, was also built at Darlington as a class D 4-4-4 tank in 1913. She would be rebuilt as a 4-6-2 tank in 1933, and would also be withdrawn in 1960. Note the station's splendid overall roof and signal gantries. *(A Brown)*

Saturday 28th June 1958. Another view of the Southern end of Durham station with ex-LNER class V2 2-6-2 No 60910 departing with an up train, whilst ex-LNER class A8, 4-6-2 tank No 69878 waits to depart with a service to Barnard Castle. The A8 tank was originally constructed at Darlington works in 1921 as a class D 4-4-4 tank, which would be rebuilt in 1936 as a 4-6-2 tank. She would be withdrawn during 1960. *(A Brown)*

Saturday 19th July 1958. During the early British Railways period, the greater bulk of the Gresley-designed class V1 and V3 2-6-2 tanks were allocated to the Scottish and North Eastern Regions, where they were used to work suburban and branch line services. Here we see class V3 No 67691 pausing at Washington station with a special train from Usworth to Durham on this Saturday, the Durham Miners Gala Day. The last in the class numerically, she was built at Doncaster works in 1940 as a V3, not as a conversion from a V1. She would be withdrawn late in 1964. *(IS Carr)*

Saturday 19th July 1958. This excellent atmospheric photograph taken inside Darlington station, shows ex-LNER class V2 2-6-2 No 60910 waiting to depart from platform 4 with the 8.05am Birmingham New Street to Newcastle train. Built at Darlington works in 1940, the locomotive would be withdrawn in 1964. Note the activity on the platform, the driver waiting for the right of way, passengers in holiday attire carrying cases, a postman pushing his bicycle and the trolleys together with mailbags. *(M Mensing)*

Monday 28th July 1958. A solitary young enthusiast seems to be the only spectator, bar the photographer, witnessing the departure of class A1 4-6-2 No 60124 *Kenilworth* from Darlington station at the head of the 7.05pm Newcastle to Bristol train. This Gateshead-allocated locomotive was built at Doncaster works in 1949, and withdrawn only 17 years later in 1966. Unfortunately, none of the class survived into the preservation scene, but the A1 Steam Locomotive Trust has built a new locomotive at Darlington using the same Peppercorn design; this is No 60163 *Tornado*. (M Mensing)

Monday 28th July 1958. This scene was becoming more common as DMUs started to replace steam traction. This Metro-Cammell built set has just arrived at Darlington station with the 12.25pm departure from Saltburn. On the right, ex-LNER class D49/2 4-4-0 No 62765 *The Goathland* is waiting to leave with a train possibly for Leeds. This D49/2 was one of the class introduced in 1928, built at Darlington works in 1934, and fitted with Lentz rotary cam poppet valves. She would be withdrawn in 1961. (M Mensing)

Monday 18th May 1959. On this Whit Monday holiday, ex-LNER class V2 2-6-2 No 60962 is seen departing Stockton station at the head of the 4.25pm Newcastle to Liverpool express. Built in 1942 at Darlington works, this locomotive would be withdrawn in 1965. *(SE Teasdale)*

Sunday 6th September 1959. Having been diverted from the East Coast Main Line, ex-LNER class A3 4-6-2 No 60102 *Sir Frederick Banbury* moves over to the Washington and Leamside route at Pelaw with the 11.05am Newcastle to London Kings Cross train. Built at Doncaster works in 1922 as a class A1 for the GNR, she was numbered 1471 and named after the last Chairman of the GNR. Numbered 4471 by the LNER, she would be rebuilt as a class A3 in 1942, and finally withdrawn by BR after almost 40 years of service in 1961. *(IS Carr)*

Friday 12th August 1960. Something of a rarity, a clean ex-WD "Austerity" class 8F 2-8-0. Seen here working a goods train at Thornaby-on-Tees, No 90434 was allocated to Thornaby depot, and looks well cared for. Built by the Vulcan Foundry in 1944, and numbered 77474 by the War Department, she was purchased by the LNER in 1946 after returning from war duty, and numbered 63113. She passed into British Railway hands on the Nationalisation of the railways and would be withdrawn in 1967 whilst allocated to West Hartlepool depot. *(EG Wootton)*

Sunday 28th August 1960. Diverted from the East Coast Main Line, ex-LNER class A4 4-6-2 No 60027 *Merlin* passes Bishop Auckland (East) with the 10.25am Edinburgh Waverley to London Kings Cross train. This Haymarket-allocated locomotive was built at Doncaster works in 1937, and originally numbered 4486. She was finally allocated to Ferryhill depot in Aberdeen where she joined several of her classmates to work the fast three-hour expresses between Glasgow and Aberdeen. She was withdrawn from service in 1965. Note the splendid array of lower quadrant signals on the gantry. *(IS Carr)*

September 1960. Prior to the 1955 Modernisation Report, which brought the introduction of the British Railways main line diesel fleet, an earlier report in 1952 heralded the introduction of DMUs for branch and secondary line work. Here we see an original 1954 Derby-built, 2-car, DMU forming the 4.47pm service to Newham leaving Blyth; the leading vehicle is No E79140. *(JC Haydon)*

Saturday 18th March 1961. A splendid branch line scene as the driver of Ivatt-designed class 2MT 2-6-0 No 46482 climbs aboard prior to moving away from Yeavering Crossing on the Coldstream to Wooler branch. This locomotive was a 1951 Darlington works built example which would be withdrawn in 1965. *(WS Sellar)*

Saturday 18th March 1961. The same locomotive and train as in the previous picture, this time approaching Wooler. The branch between Alnwick and Coldstream was opened in 1887 to provide a service to this agricultural area of Northumberland, and to tap the large amount of livestock traffic primarily coming from the market at Wooler. The passenger service on the branch was so sparse that it was withdrawn during 1930, and serious flooding in August 1948 saw a bridge washed away between Wooler and Ilderton stations. The goods service was subsequently worked from both directions, Coldstream to Wooler in the north and Alnwick to Ilderton in the south. Goods traffic on the southern section was withdrawn in March 1953 and the northern section lost its goods service in March 1965. *(WS Sellar)*

Saturday 22nd July 1961. At the head of the Saturdays-only Blackpool to South Shields train, BR Standard class 4, 2-6-0 No 76045 is seen slowing at Ravenstonedale signalbox to pick up the token for the single line section to Kirkby Stephen East. One of the later deliveries to the North Eastern Region, No 76045 was built at Doncaster in 1955 and survived only eleven years to be withdrawn in 1966. *(Derek Cross)*

Saturday 29th July 1961. Seen here south of Durham, ex-LNER class B1 4-6-0 No 61176 is heading the 8.05am Glasgow Queen Street to Scarborough service. This photograph shows the well-proportioned lines of this class, which continued to be built until 1952. This example was built at by the Vulcan Foundry in 1947, and would be withdrawn in 1965. *(IS Carr)*

Sunday 20th August 1961. With Durham station in the background, English Electric type 4 No D353 heads south with a class C goods train. Built at the Vulcan Foundry earlier in 1961, it would be withdrawn in 1983 numbered 40 153. Another success of the Pilot Scheme, this class of locomotive finally numbered 200 examples, many of which survived into the 1980s before being withdrawn. A number of the class were purchased for preservation. The graceful curving viaduct built by the NER in 1856, is now a listed structure. *(WS Sellar)*

Above: Saturday 10th February 1962. The classic North Eastern Railway heavy goods locomotive was of the 0-8-0 wheel arrangement, and here we see a very clean class T2 (LNER class Q6) No 63403 approaching Newport (Tees-side) with a train of empty coal wagons. Allocated to West Auckland depot, this locomotive was built at Darlington works in 1919, and survived to be withdrawn in 1964. In the background is ex-LNER class J39 0-6-0 No 64821 waiting with a train for the marshalling yard at Thornaby. No 64821 was built at Darlington works in 1930 and would be withdrawn in 1962. *(Dr DP Williams)*

Opposite page top: Tuesday 22nd August 1961. Introduced in 1957, examples of 0-6-0 diesel mechanical shunters were based throughout the North Eastern Region. Here we see No D2163 effectively blocking the main line whilst propelling a goods train from the New Bridge Street spur into Trafalgar Yard, seen from Manors Station platform. Argyle Street signalbox is visible protruding from the retaining wall on the left just beyond the overbridge. This locomotive was built in 1960 at Swindon, and would be withdrawn in 1976 numbered 03 163. *(IS Carr)*

Opposite page bottom: Friday 1st September 1961. Ex-NER class T3 (LNER class Q7) 0-8-0 No 63460 crosses the layout at Pelton with a Consett-bound train of bogie flatbed wagons. Built as part of the first batch of this powerful 3-cylinder class in 1919 at Darlington works, this example would be withdrawn almost a year later at the end of 1962. Fortunately, it was allocated for preservation as part of the National Collection, and is currently to be seen at Shildon. *(AR Butcher)*

Monday 26th February 1962. English Electric type 4 No D253 is seen here at the height of this year's cold winter, working the Cliffe to Uddingston train of cement tankers at Redhill cutting, Durham. This locomotive was built at the Vulcan Foundry in 1960, and would be withdrawn in 1976 numbered 40 053. *(IS Carr)*

Friday 27th April 1962. A fine view of Shildon station with a Metro-Cammell 3-car DMU working a service from Darlington to Crook. The passenger service on this branch was withdrawn in May 1965. *(IS Carr)*

Monday 21st May 1962. At Manors station, Newcastle, a train comprising three 2-car EMUs with car No E29136E leading is leaving the Jesmond line as empty stock. This stock is an example of the Metro-Cammell built units delivered in 1937.
(M Mensing)

Tuesday 22nd May 1962. One of the Hawick-based BR Standard class 2 2-6-0s No 78047 is seen here entering Berwick-upon-Tweed with the 4.00pm working from St Boswells via the Tweed Valley line. Formed of three parcel vans and one coach, the passenger service on this line only survived until June 1964. The locomotive built at Darlington works in 1955 would be withdrawn in 1966 after only eleven

Thursday 24th May 1962. Another scene at Berwick-upon-Tweed, with ex-LNER class A2/3 4-6-2 No 60517 *Ocean Swell* resting after arriving with the 3.30pm slow from Edinburgh Waverley. This locomotive was built at Doncaster works in 1946 based on a design by Edward Thompson; she would be withdrawn later in 1962. None of the Thompson-designed A2s survived into preservation, but fortunately a Peppercorn-designed A2 has, with 60532 *Blue Peter* spending many years working special trains throughout the UK. She is currently on display at Barrow Hill roundhouse near Chesterfield. *(M Mensing)*

Friday 25th May 1962. Different locomotive power at Berwick-upon-Tweed in the shape of BR/Sulzer type 2 No D5148 working the 6.55am York to Edinburgh Waverley train. Built by BR at Derby works in 1960, it would be allocated to Gateshead depot and withdrawn in 1975 numbered 24 148. Designated class 24 in the TOPS scheme, this was another of the successes of the Pilot Scheme with 151 examples built. *(M Mensing)*

Saturday 2nd June 1962. With local enthusiasts noting details, English Electric type 4 No D364 has just arrived at Newcastle Central with the 9.30am Glasgow to London Kings Cross train. This locomotive will come off the train to be replaced by another of the class to complete the journey to London. This locomotive, built at the Vulcan Foundry in 1961, would be withdrawn in 1983 numbered 40 164. *(M Mensing)*

Sunday 10th June 1962. Seen here passing Tweedmouth North signalbox, English Electric built type 5 Deltic No D9004 (as yet unnamed) is working the down "Talisman". Built at the Vulcan Foundry in 1961, it was based at Edinburgh Haymarket depot, and would survive until 1981 before being withdrawn, numbered 55 004. It would be named *Queen's Own Highlander* in May 1964. *(WS Sellar)*

Tuesday 31st July 1962. Gresley's masterpiece, a class A4 Pacific, seen here showing off its graceful sweeping lines at the head of the up Queen of Scots Pullman climbing out of Durham. No 60033 *Seagull* was built at Doncaster works in 1938, and originally numbered 4902, she would be withdrawn later in 1962.
(IS Carr)

August 1962. Ivatt-designed class 4MT 2-6-0 No 43015 has just passed Greatham station with a down mixed goods train for West Hartlepool. A Horwich works 1948-built example, she would not quite make 20 years in service before being withdrawn in 1967.
(J Appleton)

Saturday 15th September 1962. Acting as station pilot, class J72 0-6-0 tank No 69005 trundles through the gloomy centre roads at Newcastle Central into a pool of sunlight. Note the large number of mailbags stacked on the platform behind the locomotive. This locomotive was one of a batch built at Darlington works in 1949 to a 50-year old design, first introduced by the NER in 1898 as class E1. She would be withdrawn in 1964, and placed into departmental stock to be finally withdrawn in 1967. *(M Dunnett)*

Saturday 22nd September 1962. For many years after the withdrawal of passenger services on the Hexham to Riccarton Junction line in 1956, an annual excursion still traversed the route as far as Bellingham for the Agricultural Show held there. Here we see the service made up of Derby-built lightweight DMUs reversing onto the Riccarton line before departing for Bellingham. Note the delicate lower quadrant signals and posts still in use. *(MC Reed)*

Saturday 13th October 1962. All spruced up for a special working, ex-LNER class V3 2-6-2 tank No 67636 of Blaydon depot is looking particularly clean, and is seen here at West Auckland whilst working the "Durham Railtour". Built at Doncaster works in 1935 as a V1, she would be converted to a V3 in 1952, and withdrawn in 1964. *(WS Sellar)*

Friday 28th December 1962. Introduced during 1961 to replace the steam locomotives in use on the East Coast Main Line, the 22 powerful English Electric built type 5 Deltics quickly became reliable workhorses on this route. Here we see No D9012 *Crepello* passing Durham with the up "Flying Scotsman". Built at the Vulcan Foundry in 1961, she would be withdrawn twenty years later in 1981 numbered 55 012. *(IS Carr)*

Thursday 28th March 1963. A common scene during this period when steam power met diesel power. At Monkwearmouth station, BR/Sulzer Peak type 4 No D186 is at the head of the 9.42am Newcastle to Liverpool Lime Street train, and is seen passing ex-LNER class V2 2-6-2 No 60944 working a down goods. The Peak was built at Derby works in 1962, and allocated to Gateshead depot. It was withdrawn as No 46 049 in 1982, whilst the V2 was built at Darlington works in 1942, and would be withdrawn in 1965. *(IS Carr)*

Thursday 28th March 1963. Also seen at Monkwearmouth station is ex-NER class T2 (LNER class Q6) 0-8-0 No 63389 working an up mineral train. This locomotive was built at Darlington works in 1917, and would be withdrawn in 1965. Note the shunter's pole kept in a handy position on the front bufferbeam. *(IS Carr)*

Friday 19th April 1963. By this date, the English Electric built type 4s were to be seen regularly working all types of traffic on the East Coast Main Line. Here we see No D282 hauling an empty coaching stock train past North Dock signalbox near Sunderland. This locomotive was built in 1960 at the Vulcan Foundry, and would be withdrawn in 1984 numbered 40 082. *(IS Carr)*

Monday 22nd April 1963. A Metro-Cammell built 2-car DMU is seen here approaching Pallion working a service from Sunderland to Durham. On the left is NCB 0-6-2 tank No 30 with a brakevan on the line from Lambton Staithes. Built by Kitson in 1907 for the LH&JC system, No 30 would be withdrawn in 1965.
(IS Carr)

Tuesday 23rd April 1963. Gateshead depot had been allocated a number of BR/Sulzer type 2s, and here we see No D5110 passing Pallion station whilst working a Sunderland to Durham parcel train. Built at Darlington works in 1960, it was allocated to Gateshead depot and withdrawn in 1976 numbered 24 110.
(IS Carr)

Saturday 20th July 1963. Bearing a (52A) Gateshead depot shed code, ex-LNER class V2 2-6-2 No 60974 is seen arriving at Durham with the 11.25am Newcastle to Llandudno train. Built at Darlington works in 1943, she would be withdrawn in 1963. *(IS Carr)*

July 1963. Brush built type 4 locomotives started to appear on the East Coast Main Line from 1962 onwards. Here we see D1500 departing from Darlington with an up express. This locomotive was built at Loughborough in 1962, numbered 47 401 in the TOPS scheme, and would be withdrawn and purchased for preservation in 1992. It is currently at the Midland Railway Centre, Butterley, Derbyshire. *(J Appleton)*

August 1963. Away from the East Coast Main Line, steam locomotives could still be found in abundance working hard with goods, primarily mineral and coal traffic. An exceptionally clean ex-NER class P3 (LNER class J27) 0-6-0 No 65855 is seen climbing the gradient near Bedlington with a train of loaded coal wagons from Bedlington to Cambois power station in Blyth. The locomotive was one of the Wilson Worsdell designed class introduced in 1906, and built with slide valves. Constructed in 1908 by Beyer Peacock, she would also be one of the last to be withdrawn in September 1967. *(Peter J Robinson)*

Friday 25th October 1963. Just prior to the closure of the Rothbury branch in November of this year, goods trains still served the village on three days per week. On this day ex-NER class P3 (LNER class J27) 0-6-0 No 65822 was on duty, and is seen here shunting the yard. Built by the NBL in 1908, she would only survive a further couple of years to be withdrawn in 1965. *(SC Crook)*

Wednesday 11th March 1964. BR/Sulzer Peak type 4 locomotives had become regular visitors to the Newcastle area working passenger trains from Derby, Liverpool and Manchester. Here we see No D142 speeding through Ferryhill with a Newcastle to Bristol express. This locomotive was built at Derby works in 1961, and would be withdrawn in 1977 numbered 46 005. *(AR Thompson)*

Friday 17th April 1964. Seen here at Low Fell with a mixed goods train for the Tyne marshalling yard is ex-NER class P3 (LNER class J27) 0-6-0 No 65821. Another NBL-built example of 1908, this locomotive would be withdrawn in 1966. *(AR Thompson)*

Sunday 18th April 1964. Returning to Tyne Dock with empty iron ore wagons, BR Standard class 9F 2-10-0 No 92061 makes a splendid sight as it passes near Beamish. At the rear of the train is classmate No 92097. Both locomotives were built at Crewe works, the former in 1955 and the latter in 1956, and both were withdrawn from service in 1966. *(AR Thompson)*

April 1964. Seen inside the interior of Alnwick station is class K1 2-6-0 No 62012 waiting to depart with a train for the branch junction at Alnmouth. Built by the NBL in 1949, she would be withdrawn in 1967 whilst based at Sunderland depot. The passenger service on the branch would not last much longer being withdrawn in January 1968. *(Ian S Krause)*

Monday 20th July 1964. With a long rake of empty coal wagons in tow, NCB No 48 leaves the Tyne Commission Quay area in the distance. This 0-6-0 Austerity saddle tank was built by Hunslet in 1943, and would be numbered 75015 by the WD before passing into NCB hands. She was to be found working on the Backworth Colliery system into the 1970s before being sold into the preservation scene. She is currently in store at the Strathspey Railway at Aviemore. *(WS Sellar)*

Monday 20th July 1964. Having arrived at Tyne Commission Quay with a boat train, Brush type 4 No D1576 waits whilst passengers alight before it runs round the train. One of the Crewe works built examples of the class constructed in 1964, it would be withdrawn as number 47 456 in 1991. The Tyne Commission Quay was opened as The Albert Edward Dock in 1900 to provide berths to steamers connecting to the Scandinavian countries. Renamed in 1920 it would see its last passenger train in 1970. *(WS Sellar)*

Saturday 1st August 1964. The bulk of the 117 Clayton-built type 1 locomotives were based at Scottish depots, but 29 examples were constructed by Beyer Peacock, and allocated to the North Eastern Region. Working a mixed goods train leaving Trafalgar Yard is one of these examples allocated to Gateshead depot; D8592, with a brake tender leading, approaches Manor Station. Built in 1964, this locomotive would only give seven years service to BR before being withdrawn in 1971. *(IS Carr)*

Saturday 8th August 1964. The branch line service from Newbiggin-by-the-Sea to Manors via Seaton Delaval was under threat of closure, and at this time was being served by 2-car Metro-Cammell DMUs. On this day, the 4.35pm train is waiting to depart from Newbiggin. The passenger service was finally withdrawn in November 1964. *(IS Carr)*

Saturday 8th August 1964. On the same day as the previous photograph at another branch line under threat of closure, the 16.38 departure from Alnwick to Alnmouth is in the hands of class K1 2-6-0 No 62006. Built by the NBL in 1949, she would survive a further couple of years to be withdrawn in 1966 whilst allocated to Sunderland depot. The splendid station building was the second to be constructed, and was opened to coincide with the opening of the Alnwick to Coldstream branch in September 1887. The graceful curves of the overall roof can still be seen today, as the building survives as a bookshop and warehouse. *(WS Sellar)*

Wednesday 26th August 1964. BR/ Sulzer type 2 No D5148 is seen passing the distinctive Penshaw North signalbox whilst heading an up goods train. This locomotive would be numbered 24 148 in the TOPS scheme. *(IS Carr)*

August 1964. Looking very clean and smart, ex-LNER class B1 4-6-0 No 61216 is seen departing Newcastle Central station with a train of empty coaching stock. This Gateshead-allocated locomotive was built by the NBL in 1947, and would be withdrawn 20 years later in 1967. *(R Kell)*

August 1964. English Electric type 4 No D241 is seen here working an up goods, whilst a 4-car Metro-Cammell DMU is on the down line at Parkgate near Darlington. The type 4 was constructed at the Vulcan Foundry in 1959, and allocated to Gateshead depot. Numbered 40 041 in the TOPS scheme, it would be withdrawn in 1976. *(John E Hoggarth)*

December 1964. Working hard with a short goods train, ex-NER class T2 (LNER class Q6) 0-8-0 No 63427 makes a fine sight as it storms past the distant signal at Beamish. This locomotive was one of the examples built by Armstrong Whitworth in 1920. She would be withdrawn in 1965. *(WJV Anderson)*

Friday 2nd April 1965. Laying down a dense smokescreen whilst working between Jesmond and West Jesmond stations, ex-NER class P3 (LNER class J27) 0-6-0 No 65796 appears to be in need of attention as it hauls a heavy coal train. One of the earlier built examples constructed at Darlington works in 1906, she would survive 60 years to be withdrawn in 1966. *(K Willford)*

Monday 19th April 1965. Brush type 4 No D1531 pauses at Berwick-upon-Tweed whilst hauling the 14.25 Edinburgh Waverley to Newcastle service. This class of locomotive became very efficient and reliable workhorses on the East Coast Main Line with over 500 examples finally being built. The last of the class are still in operation with several companies, and a number have entered the preservation scene. D1531 was built at Loughborough in 1963, numbered 47 424 in the TOPS scheme, and withdrawn in 1991. *(N Caplan)*

Friday 23rd April 1965. Ex-NER class P3 (LNER class J27) 0-6-0 No 65831 has arrived at Silksworth with a train of empty coal wagons for the colliery. One of the Robert Stephenson built examples of 1909, she would be withdrawn in 1966. *(Peter H Rigg)*

Opposite page top:
Saturday 5th June 1965. English Electric type 4 No D253 is seen approaching Corbridge station at the head of a fitted goods train from Newcastle to Carlisle. This locomotive would be re-numbered 40 053 in TOPS. *(JS Hancock)*

Opposite page bottom:
Monday 19th July 1965. One of ten examples of this class delivered to Tyne Dock depot during 1955 and 1956 to work the heavy iron ore trains to Consett, BR Standard class 9F 2-10-0 No 92065 is seen here at Tyne Dock Bottom. Built in 1955 at Crewe works, she would be withdrawn in 1967. Steam haulage of this traffic would cease in November 1966 with BR/Sulzer type 2s working in pairs taking over the duty. *(WS Sellar)*

Right: Monday 19th July 1965. This splendid photograph was taken from the cab of BR Standard class 9F 2-10-0 No 92065 as it passed class mate No 92060 near Tyne Dock. Heading for Consett, No 92065 was working a loaded train of iron ore wagons, whilst 92060 was returning with empties. This latter locomotive was built in 1955 at Crewe works, and would be withdrawn in 1966. *(WS Sellar)*

Monday 26th July 1965. With the run down of steam traction for passenger services in the north east, several depots maintained a pool of steam locomotives for goods work, mostly coal trains from collieries to ports and power stations. At North Blyth depot we see ex-NER class P3 (LNER class J27) 0-6-0 No 65811 facing ex-NER class T2 (LNER class Q6) 0-8-0 No 63386 standing by the coaling plant. 65811 was one of the NBL-built examples of the class constructed in 1908, and would be one of the last of the class to be withdrawn in September 1967. 63386 was built at Darlington works in 1917, and would be withdrawn later in 1965. *(David Birch)*

Sunday 30th January 1966. At Winning Crossing, Blyth, ex-NER class P3 (LNER class J27) 0-6-0 No 65790 is working a southbound coal train. One of the Darlington works built examples of 1906, she would be withdrawn in 1966. *(AR Thompson)*

Sunday 6th February 1966. Storming through Norwood Junction, Gateshead with a train of empty coal hopper wagons is ex-NER class T2 (LNER class Q6) 0-8-0 No 63436. The train has originated at the Stella Power station and is heading for Sunderland. Built by Armstrong Whitworth in 1920, she would be one of the last of the class to be withdrawn in 1967. *(AR Thompson)*

Wednesday 22nd June 1966. Looking in excellent external condition, and only ten years old, BR Standard class 9F 2-10-0 No 92099 arrives at Consett with a train of coal from South Pelaw. This locomotive was constructed at Crewe works in 1956, and would be withdrawn later in 1966. *(Verdun Wake)*

Tuesday 5th July 1966. New motive power was being trialled on the Tyne Dock–Consett iron ore trains, and here we see a pair of BR/Sulzer type 2s that have slipped to a halt on the 1 in 47 gradient at Pelaw. D5112 is leading D5180, and the secondman is seen attending to the sanding gear. A type 4 diesel was later summoned to assist by banking the train for the remainder of the journey. D5112 was built at Darlington works in 1960, and would be withdrawn in 1976 numbered 24 112, whilst D5180 was built at Darlington in 1963 and would also be withdrawn in 1976 numbered 25 030. *(MF Sarney)*

Wednesday 10th August 1966. Class K1 2-6-0 No 62057 prepares to depart Cambois power station sidings with a long train of empty coal hopper wagons for Ashington Colliery. In the background, ex-NER class P3 (LNER class J27) 0-6-0 No 65811 waits for its next duty. The K1 was built by the NBL in 1949, and withdrawn in 1967. *(LA Nixon)*

Thursday 22nd September 1966. Making a spectacular departure from Scotsgap, ex-NER class P3 (LNER class J27) 0-6-0 No 65842 is heading for Woodburn with the weekly goods train. Passenger services between Scotsgap and Reedsmouth were withdrawn in 1952, but the goods service to Woodburn carried on until October 1966. The locomotive, built in 1908 by Beyer Peacock, would survive a further few months before being withdrawn early in 1967. *(David Gouldthorp)*

Saturday 22nd October 1966. One of the few remaining ex-WD Austerity class 8F 2-8-0s still in service at this time was No 90074, seen here with a train of York to North Blyth empty coal wagons approaching Aycliffe on the East Coast Main Line. This locomotive was built by the NBL in 1944, and was numbered 70872 by the War Department. She was purchased by the LNER in 1946 on her return from war duties, and numbered 63074. She passed into British Railways hands on Nationalisation, and would be one of the last of the class to be withdrawn in September 1967 when based at Sunderland depot, and the allocation of steam locomotives ceased in the North Eastern Region. *(John M Boyes)*

Friday 30th December 1966. On this bright winter day, ex-NER class T2 (LNER class Q6) 0-8-0 No 63395 is seen pounding up the 1 in 46 Seaton Bank with a train of empty coal hoppers from Sunderland to South Hetton Colliery. Built at Darlington works in 1918, she was withdrawn in September 1967, and survived into the preservation scene. She is currently undergoing a general heavy overhaul at the North Yorkshire Moors Railway. *(Maurice S Burns)*

Thursday 23rd February 1967. With a heavy train of full coal hopper wagons in tow, Ivatt-designed class 4MT 2-6-0 No 43063 storms up the last part of the climb to North Blyth staithes. This locomotive was one of the 1950 Doncaster-built examples that would survive until the end of main line steam allocations in the North East in September 1967. *(D. Mackinnon)*

Wednesday 29th March 1967. This limited stop train is formed by a 2-unit EMU, numbers E29315E and E29115E, and is seen pausing at Wallsend station. Built in 1937, they were part of an order for articulated twin units delivered by Metro-Cammell. *(Kenneth Johnson)*

Sunday 30th April 1967. BR/Sulzer Peak type 4 No D193 is seen passing Geneva signalbox near Darlington with a diverted Newcastle to Liverpool express. Built at Derby works in 1963, it was allocated to Gateshead depot, would be numbered 46 056 in TOPS, and was withdrawn in 1982. *(John M Boyes)*

Friday 2nd June 1967. Brush-built type 4 No D1109 makes a fine sight at the head of the London Kings Cross to Scotland daytime car-carrier service, as it speeds through Durham station. Another Crewe-built example of this class, it would be numbered 47 526, and is currently in store at Carnforth. *(MS Welch)*

Friday 9th June 1967. Coming to the end of its useful life, and one of the last steam locomotives still working in the North East, ex-NER class P3 (LNER class J27) 0-6-0 No 65855 is hauling a train of coal hopper wagons under the splendid signal gantry at Ryhope Grange Junction, Sunderland. *(MJ Fox)*

Thursday 20th July 1967. Ex-NER class P3 (LNER class J27) 0-6-0 No 65882 blasts its way through the rock cutting at Ryhope Colliery with a train of empty coal hopper wagons for Silksworth Colliery. This locomotive was one of the Raven developments of the original Worsdell design, fitted with piston valves, and introduced in 1921. Built at Darlington works in 1922, she would be one of the last of the class to be withdrawn in September 1967. *(Ian Allan Library)*

Tuesday 25th July 1967. Plodding past Newburn 'box at West Hartlepool is one of the last ex-WD class 8F 2-8-0s still working in the area at this time. No 90478, which was built at the Vulcan Foundry in 1944, is hauling a southbound train of full coal hopper wagons. Numbered 78679 by the WD, she was purchased by the LNER in 1946 on return from war duties in Europe and numbered 63157. She would be withdrawn from West Hartlepool depot in September 1967. *(Eric Doel)*

Above: Wednesday 26th July 1967. At Ryhope Junction, Sunderland, ex-WD class 8F 2-8-0 No 90348 accelerates southbound with a train of empty coal hopper wagons. Built by the NBL in 1944, she was numbered 77271 by the War Department, and acquired by BR in 1948. She would also end her working life at Sunderland depot in September 1967. *(Eric Doel)*

Below: Tuesday 1st August 1967. With the headgear of Silksworth Colliery in the background, ex-NER class P3 (LNER class J27) 0-6-0 No 65892 arrives with a train of empty coal hopper wagons. This locomotive was one of the Raven examples built in 1923 at Darlington works; she would be withdrawn in 1967. *(IS Carr)*

Opposite page: Tuesday 25th July 1967. Sitting quietly simmering at Sunderland depot are ex-NER class P3 (LNER class J27) 0-6-0 No 65855 and ex-WD class 8F 2-8-0 No 90135. In a shabby condition, they are close to the end of their working lives, both being withdrawn from service in September of the same year when the allocation of main line steam locomotives ceased in the North East. No 65855 was built by Beyer Peacock in 1908, whilst No 90135 was constructed by the NBL in 1943. Numbered 77040 by the WD, she would be acquired by BR in 1948, ending her working life at Sunderland depot almost 20 years later. *(Eric Doel)*

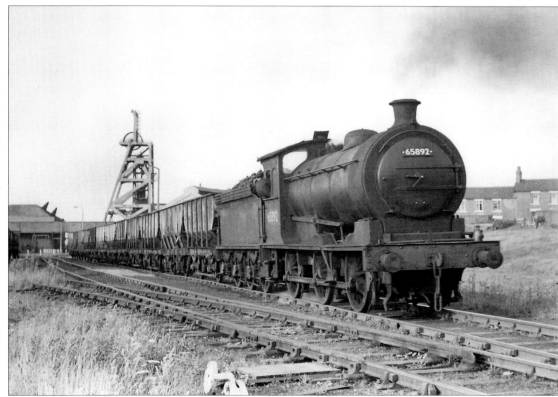

95

Friday 11th August 1967. English Electric type 3 No D6901 passes under the distinct Penshaw North signalbox with an up mixed goods train. This locomotive was constructed at the Vulcan Foundry in 1963, was renumbered 37 201 in TOPS, and withdrawn in 1996. *(JS Hancock)*

Friday 8th September 1967. With only days remaining before withdrawal, ex-NER class T2 (LNER class Q6) 0-8-0 No 63387 is seen at Billingham working the 10.05 Tees Yard to West Hartlepool goods train. This locomotive, which was built at Darlington works in 1917, would be withdrawn later in the month having served for 50 years. *(John M Boyes)*